Astronomers

Neil Morris

Chrysalis Education

Distributed in the United States by
Smart Apple Media
1980 Lookout Drive
North Mankato, MN 56003

ISBN 1-93233-378-9

Library of Congress Control Number 2003 102635

Managing Editor: Joyce Bentley
Assistant Editor: Clare Chambers
Editor: Rosalind Beckman
Designer: Sarah Crouch
Picture Researcher: Jenny Barlow

Printed in Hong Kong
10 9 8 7 6 5 4 3 2 1

Picture credits:
B = bottom; L = left; R = right; T = top.
Cover front and back Mary Evans 4 SPL 5 T Werner Forman Archive/National Library, Cairo B SPL/David Parker
6 Hulton Archive 7 T Mary Evans B Hulton Archive 8 Mary Evans 9 AKG London/Erich Lessing 10 Hulton Archive
11 T Reuters/HO B SPL/J-L Charmet 12 The Art Archive/Maritiem Museum Prins Hendrik Rotterdam/Dagli Orti
13 T Hulton Archive B Mary Evans 14 Hulton Archive 15 T SPL/Detlev Van Ravenswaay B SPL 16 Mary Evans 17
T SPL B AKG London 18 Hulton Archive 19 T SPL B AKG London 20 SPL 21 T SPL/NASA B Mary Evans 22
Hulton Archive 23 T SPL/J-L Charmet B AKG London/Erich Lessing 24 SPL/Dr Jeremy Burgess 25 T
Corbis/Bettmann B Hulton Archive 26 AKG London 27 T Hulton Archive B The Art Archive/Musée de la Tapisserie
Bayeaux/Dagli Orti 28 T SPL/David Parker B SPL/Royal Observatory, Edinburgh 29 Hulton Archive 30 T Hulton
Archive B Mary Evans 31 T Chrysalis Images/NASA B SPL 32 T Mary Evans B Hulton Archive 33 Hulton Archive
34 Rex/Timepix/Jon Brenneis 35 T SPL B Corbis/Roger Ressmeyer 36 T SPL/NASA B Corbis 37
Rex/Timepix/Margaret Bourke-White 38 SPL 39 T Hulton Archive B SPL/Mark Garlick 40 T Corbis/Bettmann B
Hulton Archive 41 AKG London 42 Corbis/Bettmann 43 T SPL B SPL/A. Behrend/Eurelios 44 SPL/David A.
Hardy 45 T SPL/Martin Bond B SPL/David Parker.
All reasonable efforts have been made to trace the relevant copyright holders of the images contained within this
book. If we were unable to reach you, please contact Chrysalis Education.

CONTENTS

INTRODUCTION

Astronomers are scientists who study stars and planets in the night sky, as well as the many other objects that exist in space. Since ancient times, astronomers have noted down everything they have observed in the skies to help us understand more about the universe. In this book, we look at the fascinating lives of ten of the world's greatest astronomers.

Observing the sky

Many people in the ancient world studied the night skies. The first astronomers thought that the objects and pinpoints of light they saw were gods who lived in the sky. Around 4,000 years ago the Egyptians were painting groups of known **stars** on coffin lids and they already recognized five **planets**. Then people realised that they could use astronomy to mark out time, making clocks and calendars. Travelers began using the **Sun** by day and the stars at night to find their way around.

The ancient scientist Ptolemy is shown here with Urania, the **muse** of astronomy.

Early astronomers

Many ancient Greek mathematicians were also astronomers. Aristarchus of Samos (c.310–230 B.C.) made early attempts to work out the size of the Sun and **Moon** and their distance from Earth. Around 210 B.C., Eratosthenes of Cyrene accurately calculated Earth's circumference. In the second century A.D., Ptolemy produced a star chart that set Earth at the center of the **universe**. This was accepted by most people for over 1,400 years.

The **constellation** Virgo, from a tenth-century Persian text called the *Book of Fixed Stars.*

Rewriting the rules

By the eighth century, Muslim scholars were translating Persian astronomical works, as well as those of Ptolemy, into Arabic. In A.D. 833, a House of Wisdom was set up in Baghdad, which included a library for Muslim astronomers. Observatories were set up, but there were few instruments and astronomers still used the naked eye. In the sixteenth century, Copernicus (see pages 6–9) was the first astronomer to challenge Ptolemy's view of the world.

Through the telescope

The discovery and development of the telescope helped astronomers expand their knowledge. Three more planets were found to be circling the Sun: Uranus was discovered in 1781 by William Herschel (see page 31); in 1846 Neptune was discovered by the German astronomer, Johann Gottfried Galle (1812–1910); and the American Clyde Tombaugh (1906–97) first saw Pluto, the farthest and smallest planet, in 1930.

Traveling in space

The first **satellite** was launched into space in 1957; the first piloted Moon landing was made in 1969; and in 1990 the first space telescope was sent into **orbit**. Together with other powerful instruments on Earth, these space adventures have helped astronomers learn even more about the universe.

Modern telescopes at Kitt Peak Observatory, in Arizona.

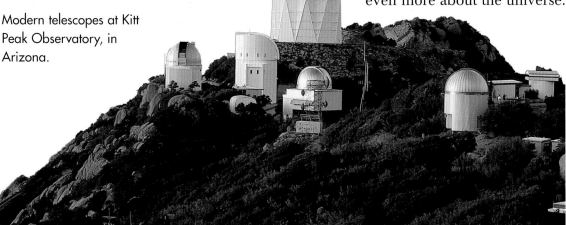

NICOLAUS COPERNICUS

1473-1543

The Polish astronomer Copernicus made the most important discovery that the Earth and other planets move around the Sun. His work marked the beginning of modern astronomy.

Nicolaus Copernicus was born in the town of Torun, in present-day central Poland. His Polish name was Mikolaj Kopernik, but he was later known by the Latin version that we use today. His father was a successful merchant and his mother was the sister of a Roman Catholic bishop.

Studies in Poland and Italy

As a young man, Copernicus was very interested in his studies. When he was 18, he entered the University of Krakow. Three years later he went to study at the University of Bologna in Italy. There, the young Copernicus studied mathematics, medicine, Greek, and Church law. At the same time, he became very interested in astronomy and began recording his observations of the night sky.

Copernicus changed everyone's view of the universe. His brilliant work influenced all astronomers, but brought many into conflict with the Christian Church.

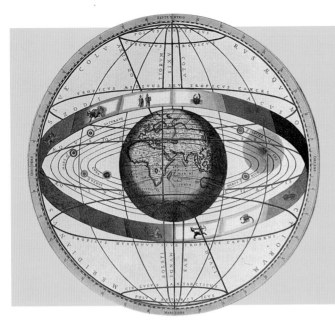

The old Ptolemaic system

Ptolemy, who lived c.A.D.100–165, made his astronomical observations in Alexandria, Egypt. He wrote a 13-part work called *Mathematical Composition*, which scholars so admired that it became known as the *Almagest* ("the greatest"). In this work, he said that the Earth was a stationary planet and that the other planets, the Moon, and the Sun moved around it. The stars were fixed points of light in a sphere. This was accepted scientific **theory** until the time of Copernicus.

Church official

Copernicus's uncle, the Bishop of Ermeland, wanted his nephew to become a Church official so that he would have a steady income. In 1497, while he was still in Bologna, Copernicus was elected a canon at the cathedral of Frombork near the Baltic coast of Poland.

Continuing at university

At the same time, the Church authorities allowed him to continue with his studies, and Copernicus moved to the University of Padua. After returning to Poland, he acted as secretary and advisor to his uncle, who died in 1512. Copernicus then went to Frombork.

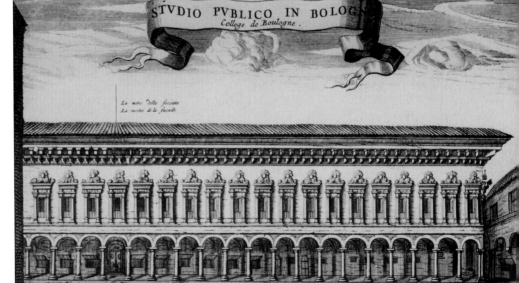

The University of Bologna, in Italy, where Copernicus studied. Dating from about 1100, it is one of the world's oldest universities.

Movements of the planets

Although he worked for the Church, Copernicus was never a priest and he had plenty of time to continue with his observations of the universe. He studied the stars and planets from a tall tower, and used simple instruments to check their movements. He was soon convinced that the best way to explain the planets' movements was to accept that all of them, including Earth, moved around the Sun. At that time, only six of the Sun's nine planets were known. Copernicus's observations led him to believe that the closest planet to the Sun was Mercury – then came Venus, Earth, Mars, Jupiter, and Saturn.

This engraved seventeenth-century diagram shows the **solar system** as described by Copernicus. The planets, including Earth, are shown moving around the Sun.

Problems with the Church

Most people at the time believed that the Earth stood still and, most importantly, that it was the center of the universe. This was taught by the Church, which believed that all God's creatures must be at the center of everything. Copernicus was aware of the difficulties his ideas would cause so, in 1514, he wrote a short summary of his findings and sent copies to friends and other scholars. In it, he also stated that the Earth spins around as it travels through space. His friends tried to persuade Copernicus to publish his theories, but he did not want to quarrel with the official position of the Church.

Calendars and currency

Copernicus was a well-read, scholarly man and he did important work in many different fields. At one time, he published his own Latin translation of the Greek verses of a seventh-century poet. In 1514, he was asked to give his opinion on alterations to the calendar, to bring it up to date with movements of the Sun and Moon. This was a problem for Copernicus because of his views, and he did not give any firm opinions. During the 1520s, he also worked on the idea of a new currency for the Polish provinces, although this was not published until 1816.

Publishing his findings

For many years, Copernicus worked on a manuscript that gave full details of his discoveries (later called the Copernican system). The finished manuscript was called *On the Revolutions of the Heavenly Spheres,* and it was probably completed by 1530. But the book did not appear until the very end of his life. It is believed that a copy of the book was brought to Copernicus at Frombork on the day that he died – May 24, 1543.

The Copernican Revolution

Copernicus's ideas were so different and so important that later scientists referred to them as the "Copernican Revolution." Copernicus expected his book to cause an uproar, but it was a technical work and many people could not understand it. Nevertheless, it did have a great influence on later scholars who realized that his observations were correct.

Copernicus's observatory in the tower of Frombork's church.

On the Revolutions

In 1540, one of Copernicus's pupils and greatest followers, the German mathematician Georg Rheticus (1514–1576), persuaded him to have his important manuscript printed. Rheticus took it to Nuremberg in Germany, but Martin Luther and other religious reformers opposed the book. So Rheticus took the manuscript to Leipzig where, at last, *On the Revolutions of the Heavenly Spheres* was printed in 1543. The reformer Andreas Osiander insisted on adding a note that the ideas were theories rather than facts.

TYCHO BRAHE

1546–1601

Danish astronomer Tycho Brahe made careful, systematic observations of the universe. These helped him to create astronomical tables that were much more accurate than those that existed before.

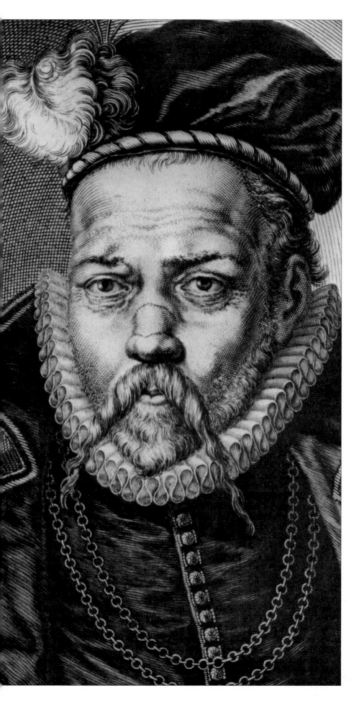

Tycho Brahe was born in the town of Knudstrup, which in 1546 was Danish but is now in Sweden. He was the son of a nobleman who became governor of the castle at Helsingborg. As a young boy, Tycho was taken to visit his rich uncle Jorgen at his castle in Tostrup. The uncle had always wanted a son of his own and decided to bring young Tycho up himself and make him his heir. Tycho's parents were forced to agree.

At college

Tycho was a bright boy and when he was just 12, he began studying law at the University of Copenhagen. While at the college, Brahe heard that astronomers predicted that there would be a total **eclipse** of the Sun on August 21, 1560.

Tycho Brache was a careful observer, who made great discoveries without the help of a telescope.

Changing star

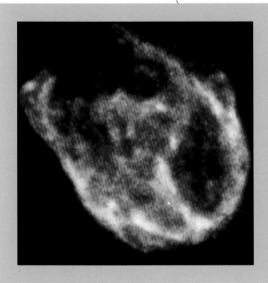

The new star that Brahe saw in 1572 was in the constellation Cassiopeia. He watched it for two years, until it faded and disappeared. Astronomers still call it Tycho's Star and now know that what he saw was a **supernova** — a type of exploding star. The most important discovery for Brahe was that it lay clearly among what were known as the fixed stars, and yet it suddenly appeared and then disappeared. This went against Aristotle's ancient theory that no change could occur in the heavens beyond the orbit of the Moon. It added to the new knowledge that had been passed on by Copernicus.

Gripped by astronomy

Brahe was amazed that astronomers could make such accurate predictions; he was even more astonished when they were proved correct. He decided that he wanted to know more about the Sun, the Moon, and the stars. A mathematics professor told Brahe about Ptolemy's *Almagest*, and other teachers helped him make compasses and other simple instruments that could be used to plot the position of stars.

Brahe used this large instrument, called an armillary, to work out the precise position of the stars.

Planets and stars

Brahe was soon studying law by day and the sky at night. In 1562, when he was 15, his uncle sent him to the University of Leipzig and there he made his own observation of a **conjunction** of the planets Jupiter and Saturn. When he looked up existing **almanacs** and Copernican tables, however, Brahe found that their predictions of this event were several days out. He decided to devote his life to accurate observation in order to correct the astronomical tables.

A new nose . . .

Brahe traveled throughout Europe and studied at Wittenberg, Basel, and Augsburg. He had a fierce temper, and one of his fits of anger had serious consequences. Around 1566, he challenged another young man to a duel, during which most of his nose was sliced off. Brahe had an artificial nose made of gold, silver, and wax which he wore for the rest of his life.

And a new star

On his travels he bought more astronomical instruments, including a giant **quadrant**, and decided to build his own small **observatory** when he inherited his uncle's estates. His new instruments led him to a great discovery. On November 11, 1572, he saw a bright star that had never been mentioned in any of the charts. He made careful observations and calculated that this "new star" was a very great distance from Earth.

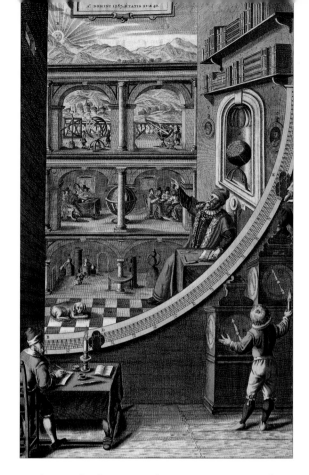

Brahe used a large quadrant to measure angles. This helped him determine the altitude, or height, of objects in the sky.

Royal patronage

In 1573, Brahe shocked his friends by marrying a peasant's daughter, Kirstine. They had eight children together. Then in 1576, Frederick II (1534–1588), the King of Denmark, heard that Brahe was planning to move to Germany to build a large observatory. He offered Brahe the small island of Ven (now part of Sweden) as a place for new scientific buildings. There, in 1577, he studied a **comet** and used his accurate instruments to prove that it was much farther away than the Moon. This added to his earlier finding of a new star.

To Prague

When King Frederick was succeeded by his son, Christian IV, Brahe's influence and income were both reduced. He left Ven and, after short stays on the Baltic coast of Germany, went in 1599 to Benatek near Prague (capital of the present-day Czech Republic). There he was supported by the Holy Roman Emperor, Rudolf II (1552–1612), who made him court astronomer.

A new observatory

Brahe set up another observatory using some of the smaller instruments he had brought with him. He had a talented German assistant named Johannes Kepler. When Brahe died a year later, in 1601, he left all the records of his observations to Kepler so that his life's work could be continued.

Frederick II, King of Denmark, was a great patron of Brahe and other scientists.

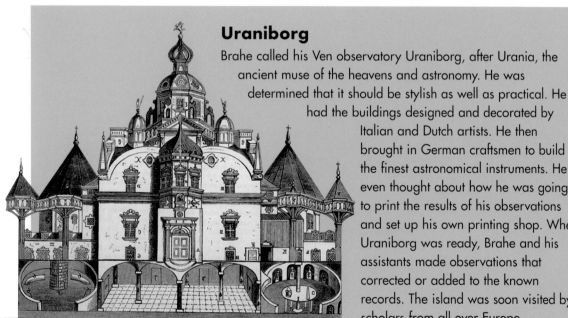

Uraniborg

Brahe called his Ven observatory Uraniborg, after Urania, the ancient muse of the heavens and astronomy. He was determined that it should be stylish as well as practical. He had the buildings designed and decorated by Italian and Dutch artists. He then brought in German craftsmen to build the finest astronomical instruments. He even thought about how he was going to print the results of his observations and set up his own printing shop. When Uraniborg was ready, Brahe and his assistants made observations that corrected or added to the known records. The island was soon visited by scholars from all over Europe.

JOHANNES KEPLER

1571–1630

The German astronomer and mathematician Johannes Kepler made important discoveries about the way in which the planets move.

Johannes Kepler was born in the German town of Weil der Stadt, near Stuttgart. His father was a mercenary soldier and his mother was the daughter of an innkeeper. The family was poor and Johannes was a sickly child. He was very bright, however, and at the age of 15 he won a scholarship from the Duke of Württemberg that allowed him to attend the University of Tübingen.

Interest in astronomy

At college, Kepler studied mathematics and learned about astronomy from a professor who firmly believed in the findings of Copernicus. This was unusual at that time and these studies influenced Kepler for the rest of his life. Kepler went on to study theology, because he wanted to become a minister of the Protestant Church. This was the Church formed by Martin Luther, the German religious reformer, who had died 40 years earlier.

Johannes Kepler built on the success of earlier astronomers. He believed in the theories of Copernicus and carried on the work of Brahe.

Teaching in Graz

In 1594, Kepler was offered an excellent position as mathematics teacher at the Lutheran high school in Graz, Austria. While teaching there, he kept up his interest in astronomy. It is said that in the summer of 1595, during a math lesson, it suddenly flashed through Kepler's mind that he could use his knowledge of geometry to find out more about the planets and the way they move.

Kepler's monument in the market square of his home town of Weil der Stadt, in Germany.

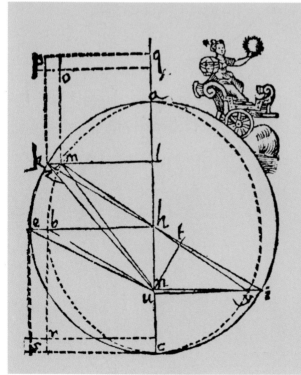

Cosmic Mystery

Kepler was a great believer in the work of the ancient Greek **philosopher** Plato and the Greek mathematician Pythagoras. Like most other sixteenth-century scientists, he followed the ancient Greeks in believing that there was harmony in the universe, as if God had used mathematical principles during its creation. In *Cosmic Mystery* (1596), Kepler worked out a system by which the six known planets were held in geometric frameworks.

Court astronomer

Kepler sent a copy of *Cosmic Mystery* to other scientists, including Tycho Brahe. The Danish astronomer was very impressed with Kepler's work. Although Brahe did not agree with all of Kepler's conclusions, in 1600 Brahe invited Kepler to join his research staff at an observatory near Prague. This was very fortunate for Kepler because, by then, Roman Catholics were forcing Protestants to leave Austria and Bavaria. When Brahe died the following year, Holy Roman Emperor Rudolf II appointed Kepler to take over as court astronomer and the imperial mathematician.

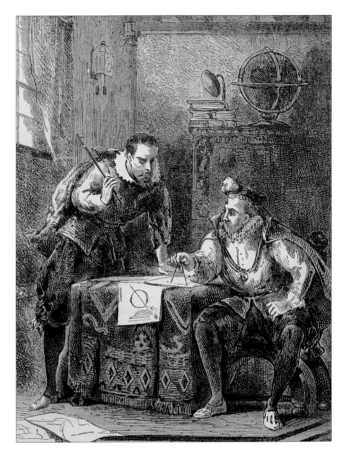

Tycho Brahe and Johannes Kepler working together in the observatory at Benatek, near Prague.

Optical work

In 1604, Kepler saw a new star in the heavens and observed its position for 17 months. Like Brahe 32 years earlier, Kepler had discovered a supernova, though he did not know what it was. In 1606, he published his findings in a book called *De Stella Nova* ("About a New Star"). His observations led him to investigate light rays and the way in which they enter the human eye. Before long, he had worked out how blurred vision occurs and why glasses can help to correct this. A few years later, he used the same ideas to explain how the newly-invented telescope worked.

Albrecht von Wallenstein

Kepler's last patron, Albrecht von Wallenstein (1583–1634), was a military general who raised an army for Holy Roman Emperor, Ferdinand II (ruled 1619–1637). Wallenstein led his troops in successful battles against Protestants in Germany and Bohemia (the modern Czech Republic). In recognition of this the Emperor made him Duke of Friedland, and Wallenstein also conquered lands for himself. He was a very ambitious man, eventually betraying the Emperor and was finally murdered by loyal imperial officers.

Orbit of Mars

Having inherited all Brahe's papers and recorded observations, Kepler began to work out the exact orbit of one of the planets, Mars. Like earlier astronomers, Brahe had thought that a planet's orbit was a perfect circle. But Kepler could not make Brahe's observed positions fit a circle or even a combination of circles. Finally, in 1609, he worked out that Mars moves around the Sun in an oval-shaped path, called an **ellipse**, rather than a circle. Kepler soon found that this was true of all the planets, and that they move faster when they are closer to the Sun. He later discovered a connection between the distance of a planet from the Sun and the time it takes for a planet to make one complete orbit around it.

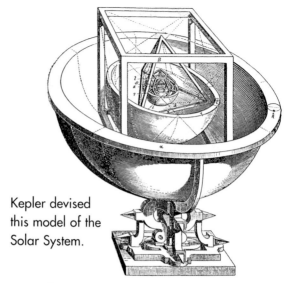

Kepler devised this model of the Solar System.

Moving on

When Rudolf II was succeeded as Holy Roman Emperor by his brother Matthias in 1612, Kepler kept his position as court astronomer but decided to leave Prague after his wife died. He went to Linz, in Austria, where he remarried.

Final journey

When the people of Linz rebelled against taxes demanded by the emperor, life became very difficult there. At Linz, Kepler had spent many years working on a new set of astronomical tables, which were now ready for printing. Backed by his patron, Albrecht von Wallenstein, Kepler moved to Zagan, in Poland, where he set up his own printing press. The *Rudolfine Tables* (dedicated to his first patron, Rudolf II) was published in 1627. When Wallenstein let him down financially, Kepler traveled back to Austria to collect money he had left there. He became ill, dying on the way.

GALILEO GALILEI

1564-1642

Galileo was the first astronomer to use a telescope to study the night sky. He made many important discoveries, including laws about falling objects and swinging pendulums.

Galileo was born in the Italian city of Pisa. His family moved to Florence while he was young and he went to school in a monastery near the city. His father wanted him to be a doctor, and in 1581 he sent Galileo to the University of Pisa to study medicine. One day, while he was in the cathedral at Pisa, he watched the lamps being lit. Some lamps swung more than others, but Galileo realized that when he timed the swings against the beat of his pulse, each one took the same time, no matter how large the swing. This was his first scientific discovery and he used it later in a timing device.

Mathematics and astronomy

Galileo was more interested in sciences other than medicine and he was glad when his father let him return to Florence to teach mathematics. In 1589, he was made professor of mathematics at the University of Pisa. He also had to teach astronomy, which fascinated him.

Galileo liked to test ideas by experiment. He has been called the founder of modern science.

Hans Lippershey

Hans Lippershey (c.1570–1619) was a Dutch spectacle-maker from Wesel (now in Germany). It is said that one day in 1608 his children were playing with some old eyeglasses in his workshop. By accident, they realized that if they held them a certain distance apart, they made faraway things look much closer. When their father saw this, he had an idea and put lenses at each end of a hollow tube. This was the first telescope, which Lippershey called a "looker." Lippershey thought that his invention would be very useful in warfare. Galileo heard about the invention and worked on building his own.

Disagreeing with the ancients

Galileo found that he disagreed with the theories of Aristotle and Ptolemy, which the university authorities and the Church still held to be true. Galileo was soon able to disprove a theory of Aristotle's that different weights fall at different speeds. He dropped two different weights from a high tower and found that they both hit the ground at the same time. Legend says that he dropped the weights from the top of the Leaning Tower of Pisa.

Galileo's telescopes were slim, wooden tubes covered with leather or paper. He used his telescopes to study the Sun, which might have caused him to go blind in later life.

The first telescopes

In 1592, Galileo moved to the University of Padua where he did his greatest work. In 1609, he heard about an amazing invention – the telescope. He learned enough to build his own version, which made distant objects appear three times larger. He quickly improved on this, making a telescope that magnified objects 32 times. When he turned it to the night sky, he saw that the Moon was not smooth, as people had thought, but covered in mountains and craters. The **Milky Way** was not just a white band in the sky, but was made up of thousands of stars. He also studied Jupiter over the course of a month and discovered that it had four moons.

Called to Rome

In 1610, Galileo returned to Florence as "personal philosopher and mathematician" to Cosimo de Medici, the Grand Duke of Tuscany. Through his telescope, Galileo saw that the planet Venus moves through phases, just like the Moon. This confirmed Copernicus's belief that the planets move around the Sun. Galileo thought that this did not conflict with Christian beliefs and he wrote letters saying so, but most Church leaders disagreed. Galileo was called to Rome and a leading Catholic cardinal ordered him not to "hold or defend" the Copernican theory – meaning he could discuss it but not say that it was true.

Sentenced by the Church

In 1624, Galileo received permission from Pope Urban VIII to write a book about the systems of the universe. This great work took eight years to research and write, and in 1632 Galileo's masterpiece, *Dialogue Concerning the Two Chief World Systems*, was published. In this book, he compared the theories of Ptolemy and Aristotle with those of Copernicus, showing that the Copernican system was correct. Galileo was once again called to Rome, and this time he was found guilty of **heresy**. He was forced to withdraw his statements and sentenced to life imprisonment.

Galileo demonstrates his telescope to the noblemen of Venice.

Galilean moons

When Galileo discovered through his telescope that Jupiter had four moons, he called them the "Medicean planets" in honor of the Medici family, who were powerful and highly-influential merchants and bankers in Florence. Today the satellites are known as the "Galilean moons," and their individual names are Callisto, Europa, Ganymede, and Io. Ganymede (left) is the largest satellite in the Solar System. We now know that Jupiter has at least 12 more moons and a faint set of rings.

Under house arrest

The Pope allowed Galileo to spend the rest of his life under house arrest in his own villa near Florence, rather than go to prison. This allowed him to continue with his work. A few years later he went blind and he finally died of a fever in 1642. It took more than 300 years after his death for the Roman Catholic Church to finally change its verdict and clear the great astronomer of heresy.

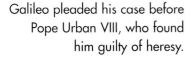

Galileo pleaded his case before Pope Urban VIII, who found him guilty of heresy.

ISAAC NEWTON

1642-1727

Isaac Newton was more than a great astronomer. He was one of the most important scientists of all time.

Isaac Newton was born on Christmas Day, 1642, the year in which Galileo died. He was born in the village of Woolsthorpe in Lincolnshire. His father, who was a farmer, died shortly before Isaac was born. When his mother remarried and moved away three years later, he stayed on the farm in Woolsthorpe with his grandmother.

Schooling

At the age of 12, Isaac was sent to school in the nearby town of Grantham, but he did not do well in his studies. His school reports described him as "idle and inattentive." Instead, he spent his time inventing and making mechanical toys, such as a model windmill and a clock. In 1656, his mother returned to the farm and called Isaac home to help her. Although he had not done well at school, Newton was no farmer either. He spent so much time with his books and homemade machines that his mother decided to send him back to school.

Issac Newton made many important discoveries in astronomy, mathematics, and **physics**.

Gravity

One day in 1665, Newton was sitting in his garden at Woolsthorpe. He was thinking about the unknown force that makes the Moon move around the Earth. Just then an apple fell from a tree, and this made him wonder what force made the apple fall down and not up. Perhaps the force working on the apple was the same as that working on the Moon? This event led Newton to work out a law concerning attraction between all the objects in the universe. He called the force "**gravity**," and the law was that of "universal gravitation."

At Cambridge University

This time he worked harder and in 1661 he went on to Trinity College, Cambridge. There he studied the ancient Greek philosophers – as well as works by the French philosopher, René Descartes, who died in 1650. Above a set of notes that he made at the time, Newton wrote: "Plato and Aristotle are my friends, but my best friend is truth." He was most interested in mathematics and physics. He worked out a basic mathematical formula for the laws of gravity that has been used ever since.

Some of Newton's papers on display in Trinity College, Cambridge.

Doing his own thinking

Newton completed his degree in 1665 and intended to stay on at university to further his studies. But a terrible plague broke out and the university was closed. Back home in Woolsthorpe, Newton spent the next two years working on mathematical problems on his own. His thinking at this time laid the foundation for his life's work – in particular, making discoveries about a force that governed Earth and the universe as a whole.

Working with prisms

Newton returned to Trinity College in 1667. He carried out many experiments, including passing light though a triangle-shaped piece of glass, called a prism. This demonstrated that a beam of white sunlight is made up of a seven distinct colours, like a rainbow.

Improving the telescope

This work led him on to create a new kind of telescope. Instead of using a combination of lenses, as others had done, Newton used a curved mirror of polished metal to collect and focus light. This meant that the telescope could be shorter, but also more powerful. Like Galileo, Newton used his first model to study the moons of Jupiter.

A private man

In 1669, Newton was appointed professor of mathematics at Trinity College. At this time, much of his work was still unknown. He was a modest man, but he hated to be criticized and never enjoyed the cut and thrust of scientific argument. He spent a great deal of time working on his own and he never married. In 1684, the astronomer Edmund Halley went to Cambridge to ask Newton about his work on the motion of the planets. He was amazed to find that Newton had complete proof of the law of gravity, including mathematical proof of the theories devised by Johannes Kepler.

The new powerful instrument that Newton invented was called a reflecting telescope.

The Royal Society

In 1672, Newton was elected a member of the Royal Society of London for the Promotion of Natural Knowledge. This scientific society had been founded in 1660 and gained royal approval from King Charles II two years later. The other members did not always like or agree with Newton, but he became president of the society in 1703 and was re-elected every year until his death. Today, the society has about 1,000 members who put the initials "FRS" (Fellow of the Royal Society) after their names.

The *Principia*

Halley persuaded Newton to publish his findings. At last Newton threw himself into this task, which resulted in his masterwork, called the *Mathematical Principles of Natural Philosophy*. Like most scientific works of the time, the book was written in Latin – usually called simply the *Principia*. It was published in 1687 and included proof of his laws of motion and gravitation. It is one of the most important scientific books ever written.

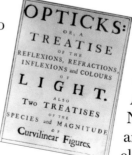

Newton published the results of many of his experiments with light in a book called *Opticks*, first printed in 1704.

MP and knight

After the *Principia* was published, Newton became much better known and more active in public life. He was elected Member of Parliament for Cambridge University in 1689. Ten years later he became master of the Mint, where money was made. In 1705, he was knighted by Queen Anne. He continued working until his death at the age of 84.

EDMUND HALLEY

1656–1742

Edmund Halley is best known for his work on comets, but he also made star charts and many other important discoveries.

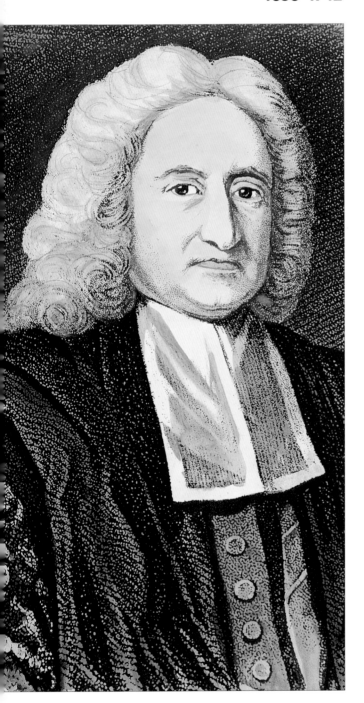

Edmund Halley was born in the village of Haggerston, near Shoreditch, which today is part of the City of London. His father was a successful merchant, dealing mainly in salt and soap. He also owned properties in London, which made him a wealthy man. This allowed him to send Edmund to St. Paul's School when he was 14, where he did very well. In 1673, he went on to Queen's College, Oxford, where he studied science.

Introduction to astronomy

While he was at Oxford, Halley showed a great interest in astronomy. Because of this, one of his teachers gave him a letter of introduction to an influential astronomer, John Flamsteed (1646–1719). Flamsteed founded the Royal Greenwich Observatory in 1675 and became England's first Astronomer Royal. Halley visited the new Royal Observatory and felt inspired to start out on his own voyage of astronomical discovery.

As well as making great discoveries about comets, Edmund Halley was able to prove that stars change position in relation to each other.

The southern stars

Flamsteed was busy compiling an accurate chart of all the stars that were visible from the Northern **Hemisphere** of the Earth. Halley decided to do the same for the Southern Hemisphere. Helped by an allowance from his father, he set sail in 1676 aboard the *Unity* for the Atlantic island of St. Helena, which was the southernmost territory under British rule. His stay on the island was not easy. The weather was poor and it was often cloudy, which made observing the night sky difficult. Nevertheless, during his year-long stay, Halley managed to record the positions of 341 southern stars. His catalog of them was published in 1678.

Observers using a quadrant and a telescope at the Royal Greenwich Observatory in London.

"A new star, a new king"

The Bayeux Tapestry shows scenes from the Norman conquest of England in 1066. One scene shows a comet in the sky. The Norman leader, William the Conqueror, saw this as a good omen and took up the battle cry: "A new star, a new king." Astronomers later realized that this had been a sighting of Halley's Comet, which was probably first noted in 240 B.C. The word comet comes from the Greek for "long-haired," because people thought the comet's tail made it look like a long-haired star.

Observing comets

In 1680, Halley traveled to France and visited Gian Domenico Cassini (1625–1712), the Italian-born director of the Observatory of Paris. Together they observed a comet in the sky and this started Halley's lifelong interest in these objects. Two years later, he saw another comet and began trying to work out its path across the sky and around the Sun. At the same time as he started his great work, Halley's personal life changed, too. In 1682, he married Mary Tooke, with whom he had a son. Two years later, Halley's father died in mysterious circumstances; many people thought that he had been murdered.

Helping Newton

When Halley was elected a fellow of the Royal Society in 1678, he met Isaac Newton and again later in Cambridge. Realizing the importance of Newton's work, Halley agreed to edit the text of his *Principia.* But he did much more than that. Halley wrote Latin verse in honor of the author at the beginning of the book, corrected the proofs, and paid for the book to be printed, in 1687.

Weather charts and maps

Around the same time, Halley also made a map of the world's winds, at a time when weather charts were unknown. In 1698, he sailed again to the South Atlantic, this time aboard the *Paramour Pink* to take accurate compass readings and check map references.

This photograph of Halley's Comet was taken in 1986. The comet will make its next close approach in 2062.

Giotto

In 1986, a **space probe** called Giotto flew to meet Halley's Comet as it made its closest approach to Earth. Giotto flew to within 381 miles of the center of the comet's head, called its **nucleus**. It found that the nucleus, made up of ice and rock dust, is 9.4 miles long and 5 miles wide. It is surrounded by a cloud of gas and dust, called a **coma**. The long tail, made of gas, always points away from the Sun as the comet travels at more than 80,000 mph.

Famous prediction

Halley, who had been appointed professor of geometry at Oxford, published a book on comets in 1705. In it he accurately described the orbits of 24 comets that had been observed by astronomers since the early fourteenth century. He showed that they moved in long, thin, oval paths around the Sun. Most importantly, he showed that the paths and other characteristics of the comets seen in 1531, 1607, and 1682 (which he saw) were very similar. In fact, they were so alike that Halley was convinced that they were all the same comet, whose orbit took it close to Earth every 75 to 76 years. He predicted that the comet would reappear in 1758.

Although his findings were eagerly awaited by Edmund Halley, John Flamsteed did not want his star catalog published until it was complete. Called *Historia Coelestis*, it appeared in three volumes in 1725, after Flamsteed's death.

Astronomer Royal

In 1716, Halley worked out a method of finding the distance between the Earth and the Sun by observing the planet Venus as it passed in front of the Sun. He also compared ancient star charts with his own and discovered that stars change their positions over long periods of time, and therefore move. In 1720, he succeeded Flamsteed as Astronomer Royal, which he remained until his death in 1742. Sixteen years later, astronomers found that Halley's prediction had been correct. When they saw the comet once again, they decided to name it Halley's Comet.

THE HERSCHELS

WILLIAM HERSCHEL 1738–1822
CAROLINE HERSCHEL 1750–1848

Helped by his sister Caroline, William Herschel built powerful telescopes and used them to discover the planet Uranus and many distant stars.

William was born Friedrich Wilhelm Herschel in Hanover, Germany. At that time, Hanover was the capital of a territory ruled by King George II of Great Britain. William's father and three older brothers were all musicians, and at the age of 14 William joined the band of the Hanoverian Guards. When the French occupied Hanover in 1757, William's parents decided to send him to England. He earned his living as a music teacher until, in 1766, he became the organist at a chapel in the city of Bath.

Caroline joins her brother

William's younger sister, Caroline Lucretia Herschel, was born in Hanover in 1750. When she was 22, William asked her to come and join him in Bath, where he gave her singing lessons and taught her English and mathematics.

William Herschel was 12 years older than his sister Caroline. They made a good team, combining their skills of observing the sky and noting down the findings.

Uranus

One night in 1781, William saw an object in the sky that he did not recognize. At first he thought it must be a comet, but then he realized that it was a previously unknown planet. He named it Georgium Sidus ("Georgian star") after King George III. When they heard of the discovery of a new planet, many other astronomers referred to it as "Herschel." Eventually, it came to be known as Uranus (who in Greek mythology represented the heavens). This seventh planet in the solar system was the first to be discovered since ancient times. In 1787, Herschel discovered two satellites, which were named Titania and Oberon, orbiting his new planet. Two years later, he also found two satellites around Saturn.

Making telescopes

By the 1770s, William had read a number of books on astronomy which began to interest him more and more, and he bought a small telescope. He quickly realized that he wanted a more powerful instrument and, because he was unable to afford one, he began grinding his own mirrors to make a larger telescope. When he started to spend a lot of time with his telescopes, Caroline helped him in his workshop and noted down all his observations.

The Herschels' usual method of working was for William to study the night sky, while his sister kept careful records.

Sir John Herschel

John Frederick William Herschel (1792–1871), son of Sir William and nephew of Caroline, was educated at England's Cambridge University. He then helped his father with his astronomical research and was a founder of the Royal Astronomical Society in 1820. After his father's death, John sailed to the southern tip of Africa and surveyed the southern skies. Over four years, he charted the southern stars as systematically as his father had studied the northern skies. He also made important studies of the Sun and was knighted by King William IV in 1831.

Full-time astronomers

Since they were now full-time astronomers, William and Caroline gave their last public musical performance in 1782. Later that year, William was appointed court astronomer to George III and the Herschels moved to Datchet, near Windsor Castle. They began studying faint patches in the night sky, called **nebulae**, and used their powerful telescopes to discover many more. Other astronomers believed that nebulae were made of fluid, but Herschel saw that some of the patches contained huge collections of stars. These were later called "island universes" and then "galaxies," the nebulae were found to be made of gas and dust.

In 1789, William Herschel built a telescope almost 40 ft long. As soon as he used it, he discovered two new satellites of Saturn.

Double stars

Brother and sister had a hard-working routine. Most nights William would observe the sky through his telescope, while Caroline noted down his observations. The next day she would organize and summarize their records, while her brother worked on making new telescopes. They sold some of these to other astronomers. In 1788, William married Mary Pitt, the widow of a former friend and four years later they had a son. William continued with his observations, and his next discovery was that of **double stars**. These are pairs of stars that circle around each other.

Theories about the universe

Unlike many earlier astronomers, William Herschel looked for a system in the heavens that might tell him about its history. He developed a theory in which the stars had originally been distributed evenly throughout the universe, before being pulled towards each other to form clusters and groups. This theory was later shown to be wrong, but such work helped other scientists develop their own theories about the history of the universe. By counting the number of stars that could be seen in each direction in the sky, Herschel was able to show that the Milky Way is shaped like a flat plate.

Wealth of information

The Herschels' observations through their new telescopes produced a wealth of information. They added up to three catalogs with lists of 2,500 nebulae and star clusters (only 103 had been known previously), as well as 848 double stars. William was knighted in 1816. When he died six years later, Caroline decided to return to Hanover. She continued to catalog her brother's findings and in 1828 she received a gold medal from the Royal Astronomical Society for her work. On her ninety-sixth birthday, the famous German scientist Alexander von Humboldt presented her with a gold medal for science on behalf of the King of Prussia. Caroline died peacefully two years later.

George III (1738–1820) was a great patron of William Herschel, who became the king's court astronomer.

EDWIN HUBBLE

1889–1953

American astronomer Edwin Hubble used giant telescopes to study galaxies beyond our own. He helped explain the size and structure of the universe.

Edwin Powell Hubble was born in the small town of Marshfield, Missouri. When he was eight, his family moved to Chicago and Hubble went to high school there. From a young age he was fascinated by science, and he enjoyed reading science fiction stories such as Jules Verne's *From the Earth to the Moon*. He also enjoyed sports at school. When he went to the University of Chicago, Hubble chose to study mathematics and astronomy. He kept up his interest in sport and was such a good boxer at college that some people thought he should take up the sport professionally.

Law studies

In 1912, Hubble traveled to England to study law at Oxford University. A year later he returned to the U.S. and became a lawyer, but he soon realized that this was not the career for him since his real interest was astronomy.

Edwin Hubble was the first astronomer to see that there were many stars in other galaxies beyond our own.

George E. Hale

The American astronomer George Ellery Hale (1868–1938) was director of Mount Wilson Observatory from 1904, when it was founded, to 1923. He set up very large telescopes, including one at Yerkes Observatory where Edwin Hubble began his research. In 1891, Hale invented and developed a special instrument for photographing the Sun, called a **spectroheliograph**. This helped him in his most important work, which was studying the Sun — especially **sunspots**. His work and leadership inspired Hubble. Hale began work on an even bigger telescope at Palomar Observatory, in California. The great 200 in. Hale Telescope only came into use after the astronomer's death.

From law to astronomy

Hubble returned to the University of Chicago and began research at the university's Yerkes Observatory in Wisconsin. After gaining his **doctorate** in astronomy in 1917, he served as an infantry officer in the U.S. Army when his country entered World War I. When the war was over, Hubble took a job at Mount Wilson Observatory in California. This was where he carried out his greatest work.

The dome of the telescope at Mount Wilson Observatory.

Beyond the Milky Way

At Mount Wilson, Hubble used a large, 100 in. telescope to look at nebulae, just as William Herschel had done with his much smaller instruments over 100 years earlier. Hubble also studied stars called **cepheids**, which are special because they change in brightness at regular intervals. An earlier American astronomer, Henrietta Leavitt (1868–1921), had shown how the changes in these variable stars could be used to calculate how far away they are. Hubble studied cepheids in a nebula called Andromeda. In 1924, he calculated that they were so many millions of miles away that they were part of a separate **galaxy**. This discovery showed that the Andromeda galaxy is completely separate from the Milky Way galaxy, to which our Sun and Earth belong.

The spiral Andromeda galaxy, which Hubble realized was a separate star system.

Galaxy shapes

Hubble went on to measure the distance to other star groups and discover more galaxies. He saw that some of these had different shapes and classified them into three main types: spiral (like a spinning Catherine wheel); elliptical (like an oval); and barred spiral (with a bright central bar of stars). Galaxies with no special shape are called irregular.

Hubble Space Telescope

Scientists realized that if they could put a telescope into space, beyond the interference of the Earth's atmosphere, they would get clearer pictures of distant stars and galaxies. As part of its space program, the U.S. National Aeronautics and Space Administration (NASA) developed the Hubble Space Telescope. It was sent up aboard a space shuttle in 1990 and orbits Earth about 375 miles out in space. Since its launch, it has been sending back spectacular photographs of deep space.

Expanding Universe

While he was studying these different galaxies, Hubble made an amazing discovery. He saw that they were moving away from the Milky Way galaxy. In 1927, his careful observations showed that the farther away other galaxies are, the faster they are moving away from us through space. This means that the universe is constantly getting bigger, which came as a shock because most scientists believed that it always stayed the same size. Now astronomers had to re-think their view of the universe.

War effort

Hubble continued with his research until World War II, when from 1942 to 1946 he worked for the U.S. War Department. Among other things, he directed the research laboratory that built wind tunnels to test the development of supersonic planes. After the war, he returned to Mount Wilson.

Hale Telescope

At Mount Wilson, Hubble helped to complete the huge telescope at Palomar Observatory, named after George Hale. He had the honor of being the first to use the new Hale Telescope in 1948. When asked what he hoped to see through it, he replied: "We hope to find something we hadn't expected."

Hubble looking through the eyepiece of the 100 in. telescope at Mount Wilson, 1937.

GEORGES LEMAÎTRE

1894–1966

The Belgian astronomer Georges Lemaître is best known for his pioneering research on how the universe developed.

As in all branches of science, people working in astronomy do not always know what other scientists are working on or have discovered. Many astronomers spend their time observing objects through telescopes, but others look at the results and try to work out why certain things happen the way they do. Georges Lemaître came up with a theory about the universe, which other people's findings showed to be correct. His ideas were dependent on the work of others, just as later astronomers found his ideas helpful in making sense of their observations. This is how science often works.

Interrupted studies

Georges Lemaître was born in the Belgian city of Charleroi in 1894. He studied mathematics and physics at the University of Louvain, and might well have become an engineer. However, just like Edwin Hubble across the Atlantic in America, his studies were interrupted by war.

Georges Lemaître was a clergyman as well as an astronomer. He combined Christian faith with scientific research.

Belgian gunners in World War I. Lemaître served in the artillery.

Soldier and trainee priest

During World War I, Lemaître served as an artillery officer in the Belgian Army, which fought on the side of the **Allied Powers** against Germany. After the war, and perhaps because of his experiences as a soldier, Lemaître decided that he wanted to train as a priest. He went into a **seminary** and in 1923 became a Catholic priest.

Studies in astronomy

Lemaître always had a great interest in astronomy and he wanted to further his studies. In 1924, he studied at the solar physics laboratory of Cambridge University, in England. The following year he went to the Massachusetts Institute of Technology (MIT) in the U.S.. While he was there, he learned about some of Edwin Hubble's findings at Mount Wilson Observatory. He was also impressed by the work of the American astronomer Harlow Shapley (1885–1972), who was director of the Harvard College Observatory. He showed that our galaxy was twice as big as people had previously thought.

The Big Bang

During the 1920s, several astonomers were working on theories about the evolution of the universe. These included Lemaître and the Russian physicist Aleksandr Friedmann (1888–1925). They both owed a great deal to the work of Albert Einstein (1879–1955), the great German-born scientist. In 1948, the Russian-born physicist George Gamov (1904–1968) came out with his own revised theory. He called the explosion that happened at the beginning of time the "Big Bang." This became the favorite term used by scientists for the similar theories of Lemaître and others. Most scientists believe that the Big Bang took place about 15 billion years ago.

Professor of astrophysics

In 1927, Lemaître became professor of **astrophysics** at the University of Louvain. In the same year, he first proposed the theory that was to make him famous. He said that the universe was constantly expanding in all directions, which was what the findings of Hubble and others showed. There was no reason to believe that this had not always been happening. So if you imagine going back in time, as if you are running a film backwards, the universe gets smaller and smaller until the galaxies all crush together into a tiny "primeval atom" or "cosmic egg."

Evolution of the universe

In 1931, the British astronomer Arthur Eddington (1882–1944) published an English translation of the notes Lemaître had written on his theory. Eddington added his own views, which agreed with Lemaître, and the Belgian astronomer was invited to London to address the British Association for the Advancement of Science. He also wrote an account of his theory for the Royal Astronomical Society. Two years later, Lemaître fully described his theory in a work called *Discussion on the Evolution of the Universe.*

Sir Arthur Eddington was director of Cambridge University Observatory from 1914 to 1944. He investigated the structure of stars and calculated the internal temperature of the Sun.

International awards

In 1995, the Georges Lemaître Foundation was set up in honor of the Belgian astronomer's achievements. Every two years the Foundation awards prizes to a scientist who has added greatly to our knowledge of the universe. The winner is chosen by an international committee of scientists and the award is presented in Louvain-la-Neuve, where Lemaître did most of his work. Georges Lemaître was given many scientific awards, including the Francqui Prize which was presented to him by Albert Einstein, and the Mendel medal which he is holding in this picture.

Gravity and cosmic rays

In 1946, Lemaître wrote another book on his great theory, called *Hypothesis of the Primeval Atom.* He carried out research in other areas of astronomy, such as the "three-body problem," which was first examined by Isaac Newton over 250 years earlier. It concerns the mathematical description of the movement of three bodies in space (such as the Sun, the Earth, and the Moon) and how they are affected by the laws of gravity. Lemaître also studied **cosmic rays** – particles that travel through space at almost the speed of light.

Proving the point

Lemaître had said the enormous energy of the Big Bang must have created **radio waves** that should still be traveling through space. In 1965, two American radio astronomers, Arno Penzias and Robert Wilson, found evidence of this background radiation. This convinced many scientists that the Big Bang theory was correct. The following year Lemaître died, and the University of Louvain named its Institute of Astronomy after him.

Albert Einstein and Georges Lemaître met several times in America during the 1930s. They had great respect for each other's work.

BERNARD LOVELL

1913–

English astronomer Sir Bernard Lovell built and directed the world's first fully-steerable radio telescope.

Bernard Lovell was born in the village of Oldland Common, near Bristol in southwest England. He went to grammar school in Bristol and then to Bristol University, where he studied physics and gained a degree in 1933. Three years later, he was awarded a doctorate. Lovell was appointed assistant lecturer in physics at the University of Manchester and in 1937 became a member of a research team studying cosmic rays. In the same year he married Mary Joyce Chesterton. They had five children.

Radar research

During World War II (1939–45), Lovell worked on the use of **radar** equipment at the Telecommunications Research Establishment. Radar (from "radio detection and ranging") had been developed during the 1930s, using reflecting microwaves to show the position of distant objects, such as enemy aircraft. This was obviously useful in wartime, but the research team also worked on using radar for safe navigation. For this important work, Lovell became an O.B.E. (Officer of the Order of the British Empire) in 1946.

Sir Bernard Lovell's name will always be associated with Jodrell Bank Observatory near Manchester, England.

Karl Jansky

Karl Jansky (1905–1950) was an American radio engineer. In 1931, he spent months using an **antenna** to try and track down the interference that people noticed on their telephones. Finally, he discovered that the interference was caused by radio waves coming from the stars. His antenna showed him that the source lay in the direction of the constellation of Sagittarius. The Dutch astronomer Jan Hendrik Oort (1900–1992) had found that this was the direction of the center of our Milky Way galaxy. Jansky published his findings and this led directly to the development of radio astronomy. In honor of his discovery, the unit of radio-wave strength was named the jansky. The first radio telescope was built in 1937 by the American engineer and amateur astronomer Grote Reber (1911–2002). His first dish was 31 ft 8 in. across.

Setting up a radio telescope

After the war, Lovell returned to Manchester University as a lecturer and began using an old army radar set to study cosmic rays. But because there was so much interference in the city, he moved the equipment and built a laboratory at Jodrell Bank, an open field about 20 miles south of Manchester. The university gave him permission to set up his first **radio telescope** there, which he mounted on a searchlight base. Lovell used this equipment to study meteor showers, as well as radio waves from the Milky Way and other galaxies. There was one great advantage over **optical** telescopes: the radio telescope could be used during the day and on cloudy nights.

A time-lapse photograph of a meteor shower. Lovell used his first radio telescope at Jodrell Bank to study meteors, which are bits of matter that burn up in the Earth's atmosphere.

The world's first satellite, *Sputnik I*, circled the Earth once every 96 minutes, for three months.

Tracking the first satellite

In 1951, Lovell was appointed professor of radio astronomy at the university. The following year he started planning a new, much larger radio telescope, with a dish that was 250 ft across. The huge dish was fully steerable as it could be moved to point in any direction to collect radio waves. The telescope went into operation just in time to track *Sputnik I,* the first artificial space satellite that was launched by the Soviet Union on October 4, 1957. Both the Soviet satellite and the British radio telescope received a great deal of publicity all over the world, as newspapers and television stations became more and more interested in the "space age."

Pulsars and quasars

In 1961, Lovell was knighted by Queen Elizabeth II. During the 1960s, he used his telescope to study different sources of radio waves from outer space. These included **pulsars** (pulsating stars that give off regular beats of radio waves) and **quasars** (quasi-stellar objects from distant galaxies that give off huge amounts of energy). Powerful radio telescopes are particularly useful in gathering information from sources very far away in deep space, much further than astronomers can see with optical telescopes. They can pick up signals that were sent millions of years ago by stars in distant galaxies. Distances in space are so vast that astronomers measure them in light years. A light year, which is 5.86 million million miles, is the distance light travels through space in a year.

Jodrell Bank Observatory

The Jodrell Bank Observatory is part of the Department of Physics and Astronomy of the University of Manchester. Its original 250 ft dish was named the Lovell Telescope in 1987. Today, it is 30 times more sensitive than when it first began operation. The telescope is still being improved and a new reflecting surface of steel plates was added in 2002. It will continue to help astronomers learn more about the life and death of stars, as well as being used in the search for **extra-terrestrial intelligence**. The dish is linked to six others, stretched across a distance of 135 miles, in a network called **MERLIN** (Multi-Element Radio-Linked Interferometer Network). This produces very detailed radio images. MERLIN is available to all professional astronomers, who can book time to use the network for their own research.

Society president

Sir Bernard Lovell was president of the Royal Astronomical Society from 1969 to 1971. Ten years later, the Society awarded him its Gold Medal. During the 1970s, he was also vice-president of the International Astronomical Union. He retired as professor of radio astronomy in 1980, but continues to work for the university. In 1990, he wrote a book about his life, which he called *Astronomer by Chance*.

Sir Bernard Lovell in the control room at Jodrell Bank. Today, the Lovell Telescope is linked to other telescopes in Europe and around the world.

GLOSSARY

Allied Powers   Those countries such as Britain, France, and the Russia U.S. that fought against Germany during World War I.

Almanac   Book of tables that is updated annually.

Antenna   Aerial that receives signals.

Astrophysics   The branch of astronomy that deals with the physical nature of stars and other heavenly objects.

Cepheid   Variable star that changes in brightness at regular intervals.

Coma   Cloud of gas and dust around the nucleus of a comet.

Comet   Body of ice and dust, with a tail of gas, that moves around the Solar System.

Conjunction   The alignment of the Earth with two planets so that they appear to be in the same position or overlap each other.

Constellation   Group of stars that ancient astronomers thought formed the shape of an animal, object, or god.

Cosmic rays   Fast-moving, high-energy radiation that reaches the Earth from all directions in space.

Doctorate   The highest academic degree. Its short form is Ph.D.

Double star   Two stars that are close together and circle around each other.

Eclipse   The obscuring of a star's light by another object, such as a planet or moon.

Ellipse   An oval shape.

Evolution   Gradual development over a long period of time.

Extra-terrestrial intelligence   Other forms of life beyond Earth.

Galaxy   Huge collection of stars; the galaxy containing our solar system is called the Milky Way (or simply the Galaxy).

Gravity   The force that attracts something towards the center of the Earth.

Hemisphere   Half of a sphere such as the Earth.

Heresy   Speaking out against an accepted religious belief.

MERLIN   Multi-Element Radio-Linked Interferometer Network. A group of radio telescopes that are linked together to give detailed images.

Milky Way   The Galaxy containing our Solar System; also, a faint band of light that appears across the night sky.

Moon   The Earth's natural satellite.

Muse   One of nine Greek goddesses who protected a particular art (such as poetry) or science (such as astronomy).

Nebula   (Plural: nebulae.) Cloud of gas. Some bright nebulae are galaxies or collections of distant stars.

Nucleus   The solid center of a comet's head.

Observatory   Building equipped for observing the night sky.

Optical   Concerning the eye or the sense of sight.

Orbit   To travel around (a star or planet).

Philosopher   Person who seeks truth and knowledge by using thought and discussion.

Physics   The science dealing with the properties of matter and energy.

Planet   Body that moves around a star.

Pulsar   Star that gives off regular beats of radio waves.

Quadrant   Instrument used for measuring angles.

Quasar   Object from a distant galaxy that gives off huge amounts of energy.

Radar   System for detecting moving objects (short for "radio detection and ranging") .

Radio telescope   Dish that collects radio waves from space.

Radio waves   Waves of electricity and magnetism that travel through space.

Satellite   Natural or artificial body that orbits a planet.

Seminary   College for religious studies.

Solar System   The Sun and all the planets and satellites that move around it.

Space probe   Unmanned spacecraft used for exploration.

Spectroheliograph   Instrument that takes photographs of the Sun.

Star   Bright ball of gas; the Sun is our nearest star.

Sun   The star that gives the Earth light and warmth.

Sunspot   Dark spot on the Sun's surface that is cooler than the rest.

Supernova   Star that suddenly gets much brighter and then explodes.

Theory   Set of ideas that tries to explain something.

Universe   All of space and everything contained in it.

INDEX